UNLOCKING OBAMACARE

A BUSINESS GUIDE TO LOWERING COSTS, INCREASING OPTIONS AND STAYING WITHIN THE LAW

PORTER T. TALBOT, MSFS

Unlocking Obamacare
A Business Guide to Lowering Costs, Increasing Options and Staying Within the Law

ISBN-13: 978-0692561003
ISBN-10: 0692561005

—Disclaimer—

Porter T. Talbot
Elevate Insurance
Address: 3160 W. Sahara Ave., Suite A25
Las Vegas, Nevada 89102
Telephone: 702-444-7283
Toll Free: 800-553-3624
Website: www.ElevateInsurance.com
Email: contact@elevateinsurance.com

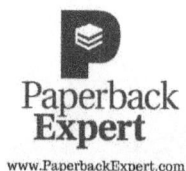

Paperback Expert
www.PaperbackExpert.com

Acknowledgments

First, special thanks to my beautiful wife Debbie. For more than 30 years you have supported and encouraged me in all my endeavors. I adore you.

Second, thanks to our five children Alisa, Afton, Stasha, Garrett and Shelly. I'm so proud of you. You are my greatest accomplishment in life.

Finally, thanks to the team at Elevate Insurance, Sea-Mountain Insurance Brokers and all of the clients that have placed their trust and confidence in us. I sincerely appreciate our relationships.

Testimonials

"With the insurance market so turbulent, it is quite refreshing to do business with a professional and knowledgeable company. Porter and his staff have guided us through a process which helped us secure great coverage for our employees and their health insurance needs. Elevate turns out to be more than just an insurance company–they offer many more opportunities that we were unaware of and happily have participated in their intranet portal. We are excited to have the opportunity to be with a supportive and caring company. I would recommend Elevate Insurance and I am definitely a hard sell!"

Sharon Cagnina
Box Canyon Primary Care

"I've had the pleasure of working with Porter and staff for more than 15 years. Their knowledge, service, integrity and dedication to their clients is most impressive. I highly recommend Elevate Insurance for all your insurance needs!"

Judy Montgomery, MBA, CPA, FACMPE
Montgomery Healthcare Consulting

"For those of us who can remember what customer service really means, Elevate Insurance never forgot, and they found a way to add a polish and a shine. Beyond that, their knowledge is on the cutting edge and spot on. When you have a question or need, they have an answer. Anyone who is doing business with this company made the right decision for so many right reasons. Hats off to Porter and his entire team."

Pat Niemiera
Pain Institute of Nevada

"Porter is extremely knowledgeable about insurance, and he goes the extra mile, which you don't see very much anymore. I feel very comfortable recommending Porter and his company. He understands the changes that are taking place with Obamacare and how best to take advantage of the new rules (including tax credits associated with the new law).

As a CPA I know the importance of getting good advice, especially when dealing with complex issues like the new rules dealing with health insurance. I would highly recommend Porter for his knowledge and customer service."

Shane White, CPA, Cr.FA
Shane White CPA

Table of Contents

Introduction

Throughout my 32 years in the insurance industry, I have always requested the privilege of delivering life insurance checks to the members of the family left behind.

I have delivered claims of all sizes, from five thousand dollars to several *hundred* thousand dollars. For the beneficiaries, these personal visits add a touch of humanity to a process that can appear indifferent to their suffering.

But my clients aren't the only ones who benefit. Over the decades, I have developed personal relationships because I left the office and delivered the checks myself. If I had delegated delivery of a check to the postal service or to an agent who hadn't been involved with the client, then I would not have developed these valuable relationships. I see people at their most vulnerable, and am often able to offer them comfort just by listening. That has been one of the most satisfying aspects of my career.

Sometimes these experiences lead to humorous moments. I remember driving up to a home once in order to deliver a life insurance claim, and seeing the wife of the deceased working in the yard. I was fairly new in the insurance business and quite nervous. She, however, was matter-of-fact about the whole thing.

"Are you the insurance guy?" she asked.

"Yes," I responded.

"Do you got a check for me?" she asked. I remember thinking she could at least act like this was more than a simple financial transaction.

She opened the envelope and said: "I thought this policy was supposed to pay double if my husband died by accident."

"Yes," I said, "but I thought your husband died of a heart attack."

"He did," she said, "but we didn't plan on it happening."

On another occasion, there was an entirely different mood. I handed an older man an envelope that contained a small group life insurance death benefit from his wife's employer. We were in his living room. He invited me to sit down and didn't say anything for a long time.

When he finally spoke, he said: "You know, this won't bring my wife back."

"I know," I said quietly.

He then walked around the room. He picked up several items and told me the significance of each one, and how each reminded him of a time that he and his wife had shared. It was heartwarming. As people have let me inside their lives a little in moments like these, I am especially grateful that the insurance money can at least relieve some of the financial burden that is added to the emotional loss.

Unlike many of my colleagues in the insurance industry, I have a graduate degree in financial services and multiple professional certifications. My education and experience have led to an expertise that allows me to write about business strategies and the Affordable Care Act.

I chose to work in the insurance business because I believe in the value of the products our industry has to offer. Although I am licensed in all areas of insurance, my focus has always been on helping employers with their group health insurance, commercial insurance, and executive planning. I like employee benefits because there are often small creative strategies that I can use to make a big difference in a company's human resource and financial needs.

Over the years, I have worked with hundreds of employers both large and small in a variety of industries, from construction companies and medical offices to municipal governments and non-profits. Counseling employers on how to design, implement, and communicate to their employees about valuable employee-benefits packages is what I love to do.

When I started our multiline independent insurance agency, I wanted to create an organization that would provide exceptional service to our customers and a positive culture for our employees. We have a great team of talented individuals who like what they do and care about the wellbeing of our clients.

We've grown rapidly in a short period of time. I think that is because people like doing business with us. We strive to help our clients honestly and ethically. We're local, experienced, and proactive.

Our agency's unique approach to managing employee benefit plans through creative strategies and proactive customer service has been very successful. Perhaps that's why more than 73 percent of our new group health insurance clients have kept their same insurance carriers and plans, and simply made us their broker of record.

Throughout this book I'll explain some of these strategies, ones that your company can implement to attain a better experience.

Chapter 1

Why I Wrote This Book

This book is for business owners, human resource managers, controllers, and CFOs who are responsible for managing the employee benefit programs in their companies.

I will provide an overview of the Affordable Care Act (ACA) and how it affects businesses, but this is not a compliance handbook. Likewise, it is not my purpose or intention to offer a political opinion about the law (not much of one anyway).

Even before the Affordable Care Act was passed, much was written and said about it. Obamacare (as it is commonly known) is polarizing, to say the least.

Proponents say millions of individuals will have insurance for the first time and that big insurance companies can no longer take advantage of consumers.

Critics, on the other hand, say the law is comparable to Armageddon. It's big government run amuck. The law is too complicated, too difficult to understand, too hard to comply with, and far too expensive.

The truth, of course, is probably somewhere in between. There is good and bad in everything, and the Affordable Care Act is no exception.

Almost every report you read or hear focuses on the legislative issues and tax penalties associated with the new rules and regulations. Very little is said about practical strategies for managing the spiraling premium costs. Employers are looking for options, and although the government has created a program to subsidize small businesses, very few employers actually qualify for assistance.

Unfortunately, most insurance brokers lack the initiative or expertise to help. They might shop for better rates once a year and occasionally assist employers with claims or billing problems, but seldom do they present new ideas.

Our agency works with employers to implement simple, proven strategies to navigate the law and make it work for you and your employees. Sometimes companies can save money on their insurance premiums and sometimes they can't, but there are techniques that can make the law work for you.

I often use the analogy of two different CPAs or accounting firms. Most accountants do a good job of preparing tax returns. They will tell you the taxes you owe based on your company's past income and expenses. I call this *reactive service*.

The second type of accountant provides *proactive service*. In addition to preparing your tax returns, a proactive accountant will earnestly analyze your current business structure, revenue, and spending patterns, and help you plan to reduce your tax liability in the future. This type of accounting firm may even help you prepare quarterly financial statements and budgets—all for no more cost than you would spend with another tax preparer. Which type of accounting firm would you prefer to work with?

Our insurance agency is proactive. Of course, we strive to lower your costs whenever possible; however, we also provide you with compliance solutions, as well as state-of-the-art human resource technology, employee onboarding capabilities, online benefit portals, and employee communications processes to improve your performance. In short, we want to help you navigate the present as we help you prepare for the future.

I've conducted several seminars regarding the impact of the Affordable Care Act for employers over the past five years, and I am often amazed at the slowness of businesses to change.

For example, in 2013 our agency partnered with a prominent CPA firm here in Las Vegas to conduct a workshop for large employers titled "The Affordable Care Act: Positioning Your Company to Win," held at the Bali Hai Golf Club. Several employers met with me afterward and said that they attended because their existing insurance broker had not fully explained to them the provisions of the law that would affect their company. More importantly, their insurance broker had not described what they could do to manage impending future developments.

Everyone asks me whether I think lawmakers will repeal the Affordable Care Act. While anything is possible, in all practicality, it would be difficult to abandon all of the positive enhancements that have been put into place, including the elimination of pre-existing conditions and subsidies for low-income households. Even if certain aspects of the law are changed, employers will need to adapt to a post-Obamacare model for doing business.

What we all need is a new paradigm, a new way of looking at things and doing things. I invite you to read this book and give our professional team of advisors a call. We'd be glad to talk to you further.

Chapter 2

Proactive Approach

66 A pessimist sees the difficulty in every
opportunity; an optimist sees the
opportunity in every difficulty. 99

— Winston Churchill

I recently met with one of our clients for a semiannual review
of employee benefits and commercial insurance policies. We
spoke about our short history together and when I first began
working with their company three years ago. Our conversation
reminded me that it is extremely valuable to implement creative
strategies for managing employee benefit plans.

This company is a successful pain-management physician's
office in Las Vegas. When I first met with them, they had fewer
than a dozen employees. They've grown a lot since then.

The practice manager began our first interview the same way
many prospective clients do: by informing us that the company
already had a good insurance broker who was knowledgeable,
responsive to their needs, and helped whenever he was asked.

The company was not looking to make any changes in what it was doing nor whom it was doing it with.

I get that a lot. It's like the adage, "Better the devil you know than the devil you don't." A lot of businesses think this way: "I know our situation's not perfect, but I'm afraid it might be worse if I change insurance brokers."

Perhaps because I came highly recommended, the practice manager asked me to review their company's existing employee benefit plans and provide them a proposal for potentially improving their current programs.

After an in-depth interview and analysis of the company's benefit programs, I made several recommendations (which I discuss later in this book). My recommendations included everything from changing insurance carriers and offering multiple plan options, to adopting a defined contribution funding method for employee health insurance premiums. After careful consideration, the employer made our agency their new broker of record and implemented the strategies I recommended.

As a result of the changes, the company has saved more than $63,000 annually, equating to over $300,000 in five years. In fact, the doctor was so pleased with our recommendations that he opted to establish a Health Reimbursement Arrangement for his employees; he gave each of them $500 in a tax-free fund to pay for out-of-pocket medical expenses. Additionally, the employees were happier because they had both more choices and more money in their pockets from the premium savings. Everyone was a winner. As I mentioned earlier, I now meet regularly with this company's practice manager to discuss the company's goals and how we can continue to align their employee benefits program to meet their future needs and objectives.

Throughout this book, I'll explain these strategies and others that your company can institute to better manage your employee benefits plans and improve morale in your workforce.

Chapter 3

A New Day

❝We have to pass the bill so that you can find out what is in it. **❞**

—Nancy Pelosi

In 2010, President Obama signed into law the Patient Protection and Affordable Care Act—commonly known as Obamacare—and forever changed health insurance in the United States.

My purpose is not to discuss all of the provisions and features of the Affordable Care Act, nor debate its merits, but rather to provide a basic understanding of the law that is essential for anyone responsible for working with employee benefits. And as most people already know by now, the rules are constantly changing. Compliance is much like trying to hit a moving target.

The Affordable Care Act equally affected individuals and employers. Here are some of the major changes initiated by the law.

- **For individuals, all health insurance policies** are now "guaranteed issue," which means there is no medical underwriting. In other words, a person's medical history is not even considered in the application process. Insurance companies cannot deny coverage to anyone based on previous health conditions, nor charge an additional premium to anyone in poor health. Additionally, there are no longer lifetime policy limits, which means that no one has to worry about their coverage ending when they need it most.

- **Individual health insurance premiums** are now determined based on a limited number of factors, including age, geographic location, family size and tobacco use. Gender is no longer considered in the premium calculations. All qualified health plans pay for preventative care such as pap smears, mammograms, and annual physicals at 100 percent. Even a fun colonoscopy is covered for individuals older than 50.

- **The individual mandate** requires all Americans to purchase health insurance or pay a penalty to the Federal government. Individuals who meet certain income requirements based on age and family size are eligible for a government subsidy to help purchase insurance through a healthcare exchange. This subsidy, called an Advanced Premium Tax Credit (APTC), is designed to help persons pay for coverage they would otherwise not be able to afford.

- **Small employers** with fully-insured health plans are primarily affected regarding the method for which premiums are determined by insurance carriers. For premium calculation purposes in 2014-2015 a small employer had less than 50 full-time employees. Starting in 2016, the definition of small employer is any company with less than 100 employees. Previously insurance carriers tied the cost of group insurance to the employer's health insurance loss ratio. In other words, companies whose employees were less healthy paid more money; companies whose employees were more healthy paid less money.

However, under the Affordable Care Act, small employer premiums are based on an adjusted community rating structure. Therefore, small companies are pooled together for premium calculation purposes based on each insurance carrier's overall loss ratio for a particular health plan.

- **Large employers with more than 50 full-time equivalent employees** (the government calls these companies "Applicable Large Employers") are required to purchase health insurance for each full-time employee or pay a penalty. This is known as the employer mandate, or employer shared responsibility provision. (In 2015, transition relief for the employer mandate was granted to companies with 50-99 employees).

Additionally, large employers' health insurance policies for their employees must meet certain standards regarding "affordability," "minimum essential coverage" and "minimum value." According to the Affordable Care Act, coverage is considered affordable if an employee's share of the self-only premium for the lowest cost plan offered by the employer is less than 9.5 percent of his or her household income indexed for inflation.

Employers can choose to pay a non-deductible tax penalty or purchase a qualified health insurance plan for their employees. This decision is often referred to as "pay or play" option.

- **Beginning in 2016**, insurance carriers, self-funded plan sponsors, and all applicable large employers must report compliance with the IRS and to their employees. Under IRC Sections 6055 and 6056, employers must provide employees with a yearly tax form by January 31st of the following year similar to a Form W-2 that indicates whether the company offered a qualified health plan to their employees that was affordable. Employees must include that information each year with their personal tax returns. The IRS will then use this information to administer the individual and employer mandates.

- **Every employer**, regardless of size, that provides group insurance must provide employees a Summary of Benefits and Coverage (SBC) at the time of application and renewal. Penalties for failing to provide this information are significant.

- **Prior to the Affordable Care Act**, employers could offer insurance benefits to one class of employee even if the plan discriminated in favor of those individuals with regard to eligibility for coverage or benefits.

  Commonly referred to as *class carve outs*, these plans have been popular among both small and large employers within certain industries, such as construction companies and restaurants with low-income wage earners and high turnover. For example, employers may have offered health insurance to all officers or management personnel only. Other instances might include offering coverage to office employees, but not to laborers; or to executives, but not support staff.

  These types of arrangements are no longer allowed by law. Nor can an employer provide a different contribution rate or different plan to managers or other select employees than that offered to everyone else. As of the time of this writing, this provision is not currently being enforced by the Department of Labor, but this situation could change at any time and employers would do well to correct their policies now. Penalties for non-compliance are significant.

Recently I met with an attorney's office in downtown Las Vegas to explain how this and other aspects of the Affordable Care Act were affecting employers. Actually, the law office itself was in violation of this provision of the law! This was because the employer paid one contribution percentage toward the lawyers' health insurance and another percentage toward the insurance for other members of their staff.

- **Another important change** under the new law is that employers can neither reimburse nor directly pay individual health insurance premiums for employees. Before the Affordable Care Act, employers were allowed to reimburse employees for individual health plans, but that has changed. This provision is currently being enforced. Although there are some sales organizations that try to promote ways around these rules, the IRS has been clear that it will not allow it. Penalties for non-compliance are significant.

I have found that this particular provision of the law affects a wide variety of employers, both small and large. For instance, a medical practice hires a doctor from out of state, but the doctor's family will not be moving for several months. Because of this, the employer agrees to reimburse the doctor for the monthly premiums on her personal health insurance policy until the family moves permanently. Situations like this happen all of the time.

With the ACA in place, it is imperative that employers understand the significant changes to health insurance coverage. Based on that understanding, employers must create a new blueprint for building a quality employee benefits program.

So as not to sound too negative, allow me to explain that I think many of the new provisions in the Affordable Care Act have been very positive. However, the big question is this: How will it all be paid for?

Recently, I worked with a woman who had previously told me that she didn't need health insurance and would rather pay a penalty than purchase a policy. Later, though, when she was in need of surgery, she called me:

"Can I buy a policy just before the surgery and drop it when I have fully recovered?" she asked.

"Yes, you can do that," I replied, "But unless you have a qualifying event, you will have to wait a short period of time to enroll for coverage."

"Okay then," she said, "I will call you back nearer the time of my surgery."

Obviously, with this type of flexibility regarding the purchase of health insurance, the future costs of the law are uncertain. Insurance companies will undoubtedly continue to raise premiums to compensate for increasing claims.

Experts often say that the term "Affordable Care Act" is really misleading. While it's true that under the law insurance is available to more people, the premiums will not necessarily be lower for individuals—and certainly not for businesses. I tell people at my seminars, "It's like standing in line at McDonald's, and the clerk tells you that you can order anything you want on the menu, and the guy behind you has to pay for it."

Chapter 4

Planning for Success

❝The best way to predict your future is to create it. ❞

—Peter F. Drucker

The word *strategy*, according to the Merriam-Webster dictionary, means "a careful plan or method for achieving a particular goal usually over a long period of time."

When the Affordable Care Act was first proposed, there was a mixture of frustration and anger on the part of the business community. I spoke to many employers, both at the seminars I conducted as well as in my office, whose initial reaction was to drop health insurance for their employees altogether.

Other employers considered making most of their employees part-time by reducing them to less than 30 hours per week, because under the employer mandate a company didn't have to provide insurance coverage for those employees. Of course, the employees could still go to the exchange and purchase an individual policy.

As an example, Darden Restaurants—parent company of such well-known brands as Olive Garden and LongHorn

Steakhouse—announced early on that it would scale back its more than 150,000 full-time employees to part-time, except for a handful of managers at each location. The company later decided against this when, in addition to other fallout, its stock dropped 37 percent, and company executives realized how much turnover this move would cause.

I was surprised when employers told me they planned to drop coverage because they weren't going to let the government tell them what to do.

To the best of my knowledge, few employers actually discontinued offering benefits to their employees as a result of the law. They provided their employees' health insurance before the Affordable Care Act not because they had to, but because they wanted to and because they recognized that it was good business.

Increasing health insurance costs and the employer mandate have significantly affected many companies, but I believe that businesses can utilize proven strategies to control the rising cost of premiums, as well as maintain or even improve employee morale. From a simple change such as offering multiple plan choices to something more complex such as self-funded insurance, I hope that you will discover ideas that your business can successfully implement.

Chapter 5

Embracing Change

❝The only thing certain in life is change. ❞

— *François de la Rochefoucauld*

Several years ago, the president of a large Las Vegas construction firm reluctantly agreed to meet me for lunch so I could demonstrate how I might save money for his company.

We had no sooner sat down than he and his controller informed me they had been with the same insurance broker for eight years. They were quite happy with him, and unless I showed them something really spectacular, our meeting was a waste of time. They did, however, appreciate the lunch.

After we ordered our meal, I quietly handed the company's president a single sheet of paper that I had created to look like a large bank check. I didn't say a word.

The "check" was written for more than $240,000. When the president asked me what it was for, I explained that it represented how much money I could *guarantee* that I would save him that year. This would be accomplished by choosing an alternative insurance carrier that offered a similar plan but with lower co-pays, deductibles, and other out-of-pocket costs.

He laughed at my style, but then wondered why his current insurance agent had never told him about this option.

After a week or so of thinking about making the change, he told me that his biggest dilemma was no longer whether to change insurance brokers—it was how to tell the old agent that he was fired.

The fact is that most of us are creatures of habit. Everyone knows the enduring proverb, "If it ain't broke, don't fix it." That's a fine proverb, but in the case of health-insurance packages, sometimes executives in a company don't know their plan is broken until they see something new. Their old policy probably was good when it was new—but other options are now available. What looks like an innovation today will be tomorrow's common practice.

After I became this company's new insurance broker, we enrolled all of the employees into the new plan. I then met with the carrier's representatives to review our expectations.

Finally, I met with the employer to review the company's experience. The president thanked me for our work, and then he pulled that $240,000 "check" out of his drawer and announced that he was still waiting to cash it. We both laughed.

Rolling with Mistakes and Changes

I'm always getting lost. You might say I'm *directionally challenged*. This is especially difficult for me in Las Vegas because so many of the houses look alike.

One day after I had picked up my oldest daughter from school, I pulled into our driveway. I punched the remote control, but the garage door wouldn't open.

I pushed the button over and over again, but nothing happened. (My daughter said later that she had never heard me swear, but she thought I was going to at that moment.)

The longer I sat there trying to open the garage door, the more upset I became. To add insult to injury, my daughter started to laugh at me!

I was about ready to make her get out of the car and fend for herself, but before I did, she explained the problem. Our door wasn't broken. It was, in fact, working just fine.

The problem was that I had unknowingly turned into our neighbor's driveway, and *my* remote control button had no effect on *the neighbor's* garage door! Every time I pushed the remote control, my daughter watched our garage door open and close and laughed.

A wise individual once said, "The difference between tragedy and humor is time." I can laugh at that experience now, but at the time I was pretty frustrated. I was so focused on what I assumed was the only solution that I failed to see any other options available to me.

I tell that story to point out that one of the easiest ways to manage health insurance premiums is simply to change the insurance carrier or the type of plan. Just like that day when I was sitting in the wrong driveway without a clue, companies can be positioned in a way that keeps the officers from seeing other options.

It seems like an obvious option, but I'm often surprised at how often employers won't consider anything other than what they've done in the past. Sometimes, they simply have turned into the wrong driveway, and a solution is as simple as backing out and pulling into the correct one.

Perhaps they feel that it's easier to pay increasing costs than to make any changes. We all develop tunnel vision from time to time and can't imagine ourselves doing anything other than what we have done in the past.

Another experience illustrates how hard we fight change, even good change. A few years ago, I was vice president of a large independent insurance agency in Idaho that had been around for decades. Like many older companies, this agency had thousands of paper files that needed to be scanned and attached to an electronic agency-management system. I got all of the employees together and laid out a plan to accomplish this task. When I asked if there were any questions, the room was silent for a few moments.

Then one of the longtime employees raised her hand and said defiantly, "I'll quit."

Curious as to her reaction, I asked, "Why would you quit?"

Her answer was the age-old, tried-and-true response: "Because we've never done it that way."

Like many of us at times, this woman had trouble with change. Once she had conquered the change, however, she eventually admitted to me that she had come to like the new way of doing things.

The way that companies have purchased health insurance is no different. Several years ago, I met with members of a law firm to discuss the firm's employee benefits program. After the company hired me as its insurance broker, we discussed the employer's goals for their employee benefits package and possible options for improvement. I suggested an alternative type of plan that would more likely fit their needs and budget objectives.

All of the decision makers were on board with the change except one, the firm's senior partner. He had to keep his doctor, he said, and he assumed his doctor would not accept such a program. So I picked up the phone and called the doctor's office. We asked about the insurance carrier and plan we were discussing. The billing department confirmed that his doctor was a contracted provider for the insurance carrier and the plan that I had recommended. The billing department further added that many of their patients were happy with it. All of my client's questions were answered to his satisfaction.

The senior partner then looked at me and asked why they should keep the policy they had rather than switch to the plan I had recommended, as though that had been his position all along. "I don't know," I said. "You're the one who said you wouldn't switch policies."

Of course, they made the change and were happy with their decision. I guess it just sounded better coming from the boss than from me.

I learned a long time ago that everything changes over time. The insurance carriers and the plan selections that are popular or competitive today may very well be the least popular or most expensive in the future.

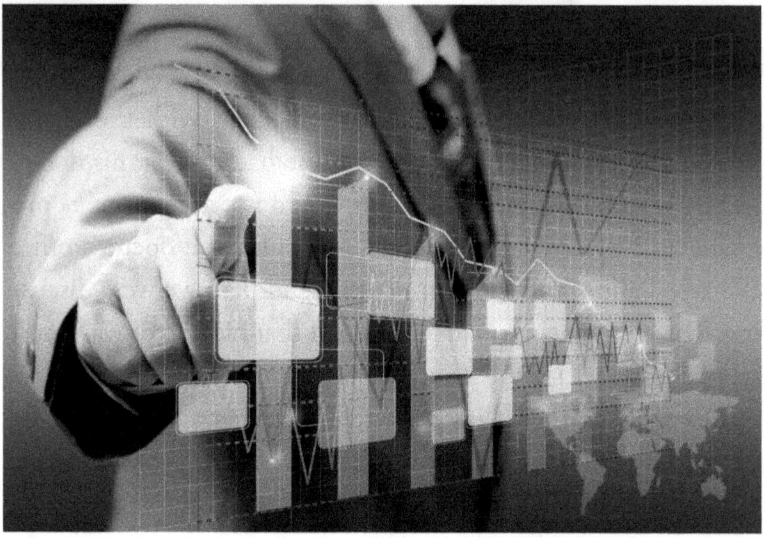

Chapter 6

Everyone Likes Choices

> ❝ As a child, my family's menu consisted of two choices: take it or leave it. ❞

> — *Buddy Hackett*

Everyone likes to have a choice. A company that offers multiple health plans gives its employees options. It puts the employees in control of their healthcare.

When I first met the office manager of a medical practice near our office, she seemed skeptical about changing insurance brokers. She had been friends with her previous agent for many years, and I could tell she wasn't enthusiastic about working with a new insurance broker.

The ideas I introduced to her included offering staff members a choice of health plans. Although the increasing health insurance premiums of their existing plan were difficult for both the employer and their employees to handle, the office manager thought that all of the staff members would opt for the better policy because of the lower deductible, so offering more than one option would be a waste of time.

However, after I presented the options to all of their employees in an enrollment meeting and explained the difference in premiums, about half of the employees selected the less-expensive policy. We are now looking at renewing their policy, and she wants to consider offering three different plan options to everyone.

Unfortunately, many insurance brokers do not routinely show employers more than one health plan. Maybe it's because they want to keep things easy for the employer and not complicate the decision-making process. Whatever the reason, I've met with many companies of all sizes whose broker has presented only one plan from each insurance carrier.

I generally recommend that the employer present at least two options to employees, and sometimes more. It doesn't cost the employer any more money, but employees will be able to choose the best plan for themselves based on their individual and family circumstances.

For almost 100 years, catalogs were a popular method for viewing and purchasing everything from clothing to household furniture. Catalogs from Sears and other retailers often showed three choices—good, better, and best. It was a simple formula for determining likely benefits and costs.

Offering health insurance to your employees can work much the same. Employees can choose from several plans with a good, better, and best selection. Perhaps the employer can contribute enough to pay for the middle option and employees can pay the difference if they want a policy with lower deductibles and out-of-pocket costs. On the other hand, some employees will choose to buy the less-expensive policy and apply the difference in the employer contribution to their dependent costs.

Chapter 7

A New Way to Budget

> It's clearly a budget. It's got a lot of numbers in it. "

— *George W. Bush*

Since the 1940s, employers have contributed toward employee health insurance plans. Most insurance carriers today require that an employer pay at least 50 percent of the employee premium in order to qualify for a group insurance policy. By paying at least half of the premium, insurance carriers are hoping to avoid "adverse selection." Adverse selection occurs when those most likely to use the insurance are the only ones who purchase coverage.

Currently, most employers pay for a percentage of the employee or single-only cost of their group health insurance plan. A relatively new concept for many employers is the defined contribution funding model. Using a defined contribution, the employer no longer pays a percentage of the employee's premium, but a fixed dollar amount—for example, $300 per month per employee. Employers may choose to contribute one specific amount towards employees and another towards dependents.

Small employers might choose to calculate an average premium, known as an *employer computed composite rate*, instead of the age-rated premium that the insurance carriers provide. A composite-rated premium is preferred by most companies and favorably compliments a defined contribution funding method. However, if the employer offers multiple plan options, there can be problems with determining the composite premium. Namely, the average rate for each plan changes depending on which plan employees select. Whatever plan the older employees choose raises the average premium and decreases the average of the other plans. Once an employer calculates an average premium for each plan, they cannot change the premium throughout the year. Unfortunately, there isn't an easy answer.

A defined contribution for health insurance has often been compared to a 401(k) retirement program versus a traditional pension plan, referred to as a defined-benefit plan. Like a 401(k) plan with a defined contribution for health insurance, the employer contributes a fixed dollar amount, and the employee can decide where to allocate the funds among the group insurance options available to them. For this reason a defined contribution works well with multiple plan options. It's like employees have a virtual gift card for their insurance benefits. If the employee wants to "buy up" to a health plan with better benefits, he will pay the difference in cost.

Employers save money by paying a fixed dollar amount toward employee health insurance costs. Employees pay the difference in premium.

One of the biggest complaints I hear from employers is that their employees have no idea how much the health insurance costs the company. All an employee knows is the amount coming out of his paycheck, not the amount the employer has paid. A defined contribution makes the employer's payment transparent. Additionally, a defined contribution method makes annual premium increases easier to manage. Employees no longer expect the employer to pick up all or most of the increase every year. If the employer had always paid 100 percent of the premium, the employee might expect his company to continue doing so. Anything less would seem like the employer had cut back on the company's contribution. With a defined-contribution method, it is easy for the employer to budget – $350 per employee this year, maybe $400 next year, and so forth.

Another key advantage for employers regarding defined contribution funding is that it gives employees some "skin in the game" because they are financially connected to the cost of the insurance. In other words, the employees have a better appreciation of the total expense.

Large employers must be careful to contribute enough toward the cost of the single-only premium of the least-expensive plan they offer so that the plan meets the affordability test for all employees. Otherwise, they may be subject to tax penalties as previously mentioned.

Chapter 8

It's Your Money

“The safe way to double your
money is to fold it over once and
put it in your pocket. ”

—Frank McKinney Hubbard

Health Savings Accounts have been around for more than
a decade, and have grown rapidly in popularity since the
Affordable Care Act became law. However, a lot of employers
are still not aware of how these types of policies can work within
their overall employee-benefits strategy.

In order to contribute to a Health Savings Account, an individual must purchase a qualified High Deductible Health Plan
(HDHP). The primary difference between an HDHP and a PPO
policy is that HDHPs do not have co-pays for doctor's office visits
or prescription drugs; instead, all out-of-pocket medical expenses
are applied towards the calendar year deductible. Preventative
care is covered at 100 percent.

Because there are no co-pays for certain types of medical care,
premiums for qualified HDHPs are generally less expensive than

other medical insurance policies, which saves money for the employer and employees. Additionally, individuals with these plans receive the insurance carrier's negotiated provider discounts for medical procedures and prescription drugs. If you've ever paid attention to the "explanation of benefits" statements you have received from a health insurance carrier, these provider discounts can be anywhere from *30 percent to 70 percent off* the original charge.

> Employers save money by purchasing an HSA qualified high deductible health plan in which all expenses (including office visits and prescription drugs) accumulate towards the annual deductible.

Those who have purchased a qualified High Deductible Health Plan may contribute towards a tax-advantaged Health Savings Account (HSA). In 2016, the maximum annual contribution to an HSA for an individual plan is $3,350 and for a family plan is $6,750. People older than 55 may contribute an additional $1,000 annually. Participants are provided debit cards to access the funds.

Either an employer or an employee can contribute to an HSA, which offers three tax advantages. First, all contributions are tax-deductible, meaning that any contributions made to an HSA lower a person's taxable income. Second, growth on earnings is tax-deferred. This feature allows your money to grow faster since every dollar is earning interest. Third, distributions for qualified medical, dental, or vision expenses are tax-free.

Unlike a flexible spending account, an HSA is not "use it or lose it" but allows unused funds to roll over from year to year. There is a penalty for withdrawing funds for nonqualified expenses prior to age 65, and for this reason, some experts have referred to these accounts as "medical IRAs."

My wife and I have had a Health Savings Account for many years. When our children were younger, our family was pretty healthy, and so we generally didn't have a lot of medical expenses. We contributed to an HSA and used the money for orthodontic expenses.

Now that our children no longer live with us, we still like having a qualified High Deductible Health Plan and Health Savings Account for the premium savings and tax benefits. As an employer, we currently pay a defined contribution for each employee and offer a choice between a Gold Option PPO and an HSA for all full-time team members. By opting for a qualified High Deductible Health Plan, my wife and I save more than $5,900 annually, and we put our premium savings into a tax-advantaged Health Savings Account.

As I mentioned earlier, the Affordable Care Act no longer allows employers to reimburse employees for their individual health insurance premiums, and the penalty for violating this law is substantial. However, an employer can contribute to an employee's HSA.

Not long ago, I received a referral from another insurance agency to a company that wanted to help its employees pay for health care, but didn't feel it could afford the required 50 percent contribution for obtaining group insurance.

We presented a unique option to this employer that allowed many of the employees to qualify for a subsidy to help pay for their insurance and the employer to contribute to their Health Savings Accounts. Our team met with their employees and helped those who were interested to purchase qualified High Deductible

Health Plans, both on and off the state exchange. Some individuals had almost their entire monthly premium paid through an Advanced Premium Tax Credit because of their income and family size.

For employees who did purchase policies, the employer contributed $100 per month to their HSA. As a result, the employees have health insurance and funds available to cover much of the out-of-pocket expense.

Chapter 9

Deductible Buy-Down

66 When employees are happy, they are your best ambassadors. 99

—James Sinegal

A Health Reimbursement Arrangement (HRA) is a plan that enables the employer to reimburse an employee enrolled in the group medical insurance for a portion of his deductible or co-insurance charges. These plans are sometimes referred to as deductible buy-down programs. Unlike a Health Savings Account (HSA), an HRA works with any type of health insurance policy and is always funded by the employer.

A few years ago, I was the insurance broker for a city in southeast Idaho. By making some changes to the city's health insurance policy, they were able to save money on premiums and encourage their employees to practice healthful lifestyles.

As part of its corporate wellness program, the city wanted each employee to obtain a physical exam. Of course, all health plans today pay 100 percent for preventative care, as required by the Affordable Care Act, so the employees' only real cost would be the time spent at the doctor's office.

You're probably aware that there are two ways to motivate people: the carrot and the stick. Initially, the city's chief financial officer wanted to penalize those who failed to get an annual physical by charging them a higher share of the premium than other employees who obtained an exam. In other words, the city would use the stick method.

I suggested an alternative option that offered a carrot: a Health Reimbursement Arrangement, wherein the employer would charge *all* of the employees the higher premium and contribute money to the employee's HRA for anyone who went for the exam.

I think most people would prefer an incentive for success rather than a penalty for failure. Agreeing with me, the city set up an HRA program and used a qualified third-party administrator that I recommended for compliance purposes. For each employee who went for a physical exam during the year, the city contributed $750 annually plus an additional $750 for the employee's spouse—a total of $1,500. Imagine the good will the city created by paying employees to do something they knew they should do anyway! The program generated a lot of excitement.

The results were impressive. By the end of the first plan year, more than 80 percent of employees got a physical exam, which was the original purpose of the corporate wellness program. Moreover, the city's human resource director informed me that several employees' doctors had discovered a medical condition during the exam that they were not previously aware of, such as high blood pressure or diabetes. These employees were now seeking treatment.

Health Reimbursement Arrangements also work well if employers are changing from a low deductible to a higher deductible. For instance, if the employer is going from a $500 to a $1,500 calendar-year deductible, the employer can return some of the premium savings to employees through an HRA. In this example, the employer's maximum liability is $1,000 per employee. Therefore, if the employer saves more than $80 per month, per employee, the company is guaranteed to reduce their health insurance expenses.

> $1,500 Calendar Year Deductible
> – $1,000 Employer reimbursement
> = $500 Employee pays

Of course, not every employee will need to be reimbursed the full amount of their deductible every year. According to a brochure for United Healthcare, based on a national sample of small-business claims data for fully insured plans in 2011, *60 percent of employees spend less than $1,500 annually in health-care expenses.* This means that the employer might only have to reimburse 40 percent of employees' deductibles!

Like a Health Savings Account, a Health Reimbursement Arrangement offers substantial tax advantages. Company contributions to employees' HRA plans are tax deductible to the business, and employees do not recognize the contributions as taxable income.

> Employers save money by purchasing any high deductible health plan and reimbursing employees for expenses that exceed a lower deductible.

Health Reimbursement Arrangements are flexible. Employers can decide to reimburse deductible only, deductibles and co-insurance, or all medical expenses—including those of the employee's family. Generally, an explanation of benefits is required to substantiate qualified expenses.

If the Health Reimbursement Arrangement is prefunded, any unused money may roll over from year to year. However, unlike HSAs, employers keep what is left in the employee's Health Reimbursement Arrangement at the termination of employment.

Employees also like a Health Reimbursement Arrangement because they see the cash deposited into their account. Most insurance plans pay the provider directly; while this offers convenience, the employee never actually sees the money. And people like to see the money.

Chapter 10

Ultimate Control

66 Control your own destiny, or
someone else will. 99

—*Jack Welch*

I once asked the chief financial officer of a midsize company how much his firm spent on health insurance each year. He knew without looking at a report.

"About $248,000," he said.

"How much of that money went to pay claims?" I asked him.

"I have no idea," he said and smiled.

I then asked him to name a single other item on the company's profit-and-loss statement with costs close to a quarter of a million dollars that he had *absolutely no idea where the money went.*

He couldn't do it.

For some reason, companies seem to be willing to pay hundreds of thousands of dollars on health insurance without knowing how much of that money is actually used to pay for the health-related expenses of their employees.

One solution to this problem is self-funded health plans. Self-funded health plans are certainly my favorite strategy for managing the rising cost of premiums. This won't work for every employer; but when it fits, self-funding can be a powerful tool that gives employers the ultimate control over their company's health-care expenditures.

People think only large employers like the MGM Grand can self-fund health insurance, companies that could handle a million-dollar claim. And it's true that the majority of all large companies self-fund their health insurance benefits. However, self-funding is now becoming popular with companies with as few as 25 employees. According to a 2014 CIGNA Insurance Company white paper titled *Advantages and Myths of Self-funding for Employers With Fewer Than 250 Employees*, "Smaller employers can be hesitant to self-fund a health plan because such plans are perceived as only appropriate for large employers. However, there exists new and innovative products and services specifically designed for employers with fewer than 250 employees that can make a self-funded health plan a compelling option for employers with as few as 25 employees."[1]

A self-funded health insurance plan is like a hybrid between a fully-insured and a self-insured policy. Like a fully-insured policy, in a properly arranged self-funded policy the employer has a certain annual premium for one year. In other words, following the initial medical underwriting process, the insurance carrier or qualified third party administrator guarantees the cost of the

1 http://www.cigna.com/assets/docs/employers-and-organizations/small-business-health-insurance-plans.pdf

final premium for 12 months. Risk is eliminated with stop-loss insurance to cover large claims. This means that the employer can have confidence that costs will not increase during the policy term. Like a self-insured policy, the employer has the possibility of getting money back if claims incurred during the annual plan year are less than expected. Therefore, a self-funded plan may have *no chance of loss and every probability of gain.*

Let's use the example of ABC Electric. In this illustration we'll assume the company has 100 employees to be insured, and the monthly self-funded health insurance premium is $300 per employee. The total annual premium, therefore, is $360,000. That premium is guaranteed for 12 months. In other words, the premium cannot be increased during the one-year term of the policy—regardless of the severity or frequency of the employee's claims.

As mentioned, each self-funded health insurance plan is medically underwritten, and the costs of the premiums are actuarially determined based on the company's past and anticipated claims experience. The premium collected by the third party administrator is divided into three different components. First, a portion goes towards the cost of administration; second, another portion of the premium is used to purchase stop-loss insurance coverage; and third, the balance of the premium is set aside in a bank account to pay future health claims. It is no different than a traditional or fully insured health insurance policy, except that the components are unbundled so that the employer can see where the money is going.

Let's suppose that one-third of ABC Electric's annual premium—$120,000—is used to pay for administrative expenses and a stop-loss insurance policy. That leaves $240,000 to be deposited into a trust account to pay claims; we will call this the *claims fund.*

> ABC Electric (Example)
>
> $120,000 Administration/Stop loss policy
> +240,000 Employer's Claims Fund
> $360,000 Total Annual Premium
>
> $15,000 Specific deductible
> $240,000 Aggregate deductible

Is it possible an employer may have health insurance claims exceeding the $240,000 in their claims fund? Absolutely. So then what?

Each self-funded insurance plan with stop-loss insurance has two built-in protections that serve to eliminate risk: the specific deductible and the aggregate deductible.

The specific deductible protects the employer from any one employee or dependent with large medical expenses. For example, if the self-funded plan had a specific deductible of $15,000, only $15,000 for any one individual's claims counts towards the employer's claims fund. The stop-loss policy pays for the rest of the person's claims.

Of course, there could be a situation in which multiple employees have large claims of more than the policy's specific deductible, or collectively there are enough small claims to exhaust the claims fund. That's where the aggregate deductible comes into play. If at any time the total incurred claims by all persons insured exceed the amount set aside in the claims fund, the stop-loss insurance pays the balance.

Self-funded Health Insurance Plan

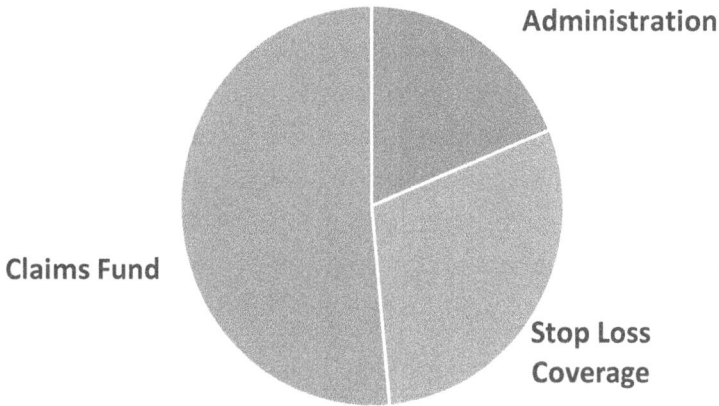

Administration

Claims Fund

Stop Loss Coverage

I'm sometimes asked: "If there is no money in the claims fund at the end of the plan year and the stop-loss insurance has had to pay out money, will the employer see a premium increase the next year?" The answer is yes. In fact, the premium probably will go up every year because of health care inflation, even if the health claims do not exhaust the claims fund. In that sense, self-funding is typically no different than a traditional insurance policy.

Employers save money by purchasing an unbundled health plan with premium guarantees and share in any unused claims funds.

So what's the advantage of a self-funded health insurance policy? The advantage is the potential to get some of the premium returned in years that health claims are less than originally projected. Suppose in the example of ABC Electric, the company pays out only $100,000 of the $240,000 available in the claims fund. Who gets the rest of the money? The employer does. (It must be noted that there is a usual delay of between 12 and 18 months set-aside for claims to be paid that were incurred but not reported during the plan year.)

In addition to the possibility of a return of any money left over in the claims fund, employers like self-funded policies because the company receives periodic claims reports that show all their claims, deposits, and withdrawals. I've had employers tell me they wouldn't even care if the company didn't get any money back at the end of the year, as long as they knew that the premium they paid went towards their employees' health care.

Remember the CFO who had no idea how much money his insurance carrier spent on health claims? With self-funding, an employer knows exactly where he stands and whether he has money coming back at the end of the plan year. The claims reports often detail how much money was spent for medical expenses such as physicians' visits, prescription drugs, and hospitalization. Of course, patients' names are not disclosed for privacy reasons.

Another huge benefit of self-funding is that each employer's plan is medically underwritten based on the company's own employees claims experience rather than the adjusted community rating structure imposed on small employers by the Affordable Care Act. Companies with healthy employees are therefore rewarded with lower premiums, and employers are more likely to implement corporate wellness programs that promote healthful lifestyles on the part of their workforce.

For this reason, industry experts have speculated that the government will seek to limit small employers from self-funding, because some employers will benefit from underwriting their company's risk. Specifically, the concern is that healthy employers (those with lower health-insurance claims) will opt for self-funding and leave the fully insured plans subject to the adjusted community rating structure. This would create an imbalance in the adjusted community rating structure and therefore affect the overall success of the Affordable Care Act.

Instances of small-business self-funding restriction already exist. For instance, in January 2015 the mayor of the District of Columbia signed into law the *Federal Health Reform Implementation and Omnibus Amendment Act*, which limited employers of certain sizes in the District from purchasing stop-loss insurance—thus restricting small employers from self-funding.

For years, employers of all sizes have emphasized workplace safety to reduce worker compensation claims; now, employers have an incentive to emphasize corporate wellness programs to similarly reduce health-insurance claims. The lower the claims, the lower the premiums.

My experience with self-funding began about 20 years ago when I helped an actor in New York set up a plan for his production company. A business consultant for this actor had heard about my work in the employee benefits industry and recommended me as one of several insurance agents to make a presentation.

I was asked to submit my written proposal, but no one told me who the actor was. I knew only that he had been in several action films and was very interested in health and wellness. He wanted a plan that would emphasize an active lifestyle. He appreciated a holistic approach to medicine with things such as Chinese acupuncture and other nontraditional medical procedures.

I chose to present a self-funded health plan that would provide his company with the possibility of reducing its long-term health insurance costs, provide detailed reporting, and support the company's wellness goals. His company could institute incentives to keep employees healthy.

When we arrived in New York City, I still didn't know who the actor was. His business consultant was quite arrogant and told me more than once to hide my excitement when I met the man. I was not to ask for an autograph or in any way indicate that my presentation was anything more than a routine proposal.

Apparently, three other insurance brokers had already made presentations. After I concluded presenting my proposal, the consultant said the company had chosen me as its new broker of record. I respectfully thanked him for the opportunity to present, and assured him that the company's trust was well founded.

Then he asked why I didn't seem too excited. I reminded him that he had instructed me not to be excited! It was a confusing experience, to say the least.

I worked with the production company's human resources director. Every quarter, I analyzed their company's claims reports and discussed the progress of the self-funded plan toward reaching their corporate financial and wellness goals.

The self-funded health insurance plan worked very well for several years…right up until the actor went to jail for personal tax evasion.

Of course, this is just a brief overview of self-funding. It is important that an employer understand all of the features and regulatory issues of this unique health insurance product before purchasing a policy. An employer would discuss these issues, as well as receive answers to any specific questions, during the presentation of our proposal.

Self-funding can make sense for many companies, including smaller employers. It can save companies money, offer flexible plan designs, provide valuable reporting, and give incentives to increase healthful behavior. My experience has been that few insurance brokers are discussing self-funded health plans with their clients. It's a shame, because it can be a terrific option for many companies.

Chapter 11

Complete Package

Not long ago one of my sons-in-law decided to change employers. The annual salary of his former company and of the new one was about the same. However, there was a large difference in the overall benefits package, which was one of the primary factors that influenced his decision to change jobs.

When he returned from his interview that evening, he proudly showed me his offer of employment from the new firm, which included only one sentence about salary. The rest of the document highlighted all of the other benefits of working for their company, with special emphasis on their comprehensive employee benefits package.

My experience indicates that many employees value non-medical benefits such as group life, dental, vision, and disability income insurance as much or more than health insurance. Perhaps it's because we don't often appreciate the worth of health insurance until we become sick or injured and need the coverage. In other words, a person doesn't see the immediate value of the health insurance that he's paying for; contrast this with insurance products such as dental coverage, which might be used more often.

Moreover, perhaps due to the challenges of today's economy, many employers are implementing voluntary benefit programs for their workforce. In these voluntary benefit programs, companies allow their employees to purchase group insurance products or supplemental benefits (such as accident or critical illness insurance) through the convenience of payroll deduction. Although the employers may not be contributing financially, the employee receives group insurance discounts and has access to financial products that might not otherwise be available individually.

I think employees may view the size or scope of the overall benefits package as a measure of the value the employer places on their worth as an employee. Studies have shown that it is vitally important for companies to ensure that employees know how much money the company invests in employee benefits; otherwise, the employees will not appreciate the employer's commitment to the workforce.

One way to share this information is with an annual benefit statement that itemizes the company's contribution to government-required expenses (such as Social Security taxes and workers' compensation insurance) as well as voluntary employer-funded programs including health, life, dental and vision insurance. A benefit statement could also list items such as vacation and sick pay, company vehicle allowances, and any other employer-paid benefits. These items are often referred to as the employee's "hidden paycheck" because the items aren't part of the employee's hourly wage or salary, but still represent a contribution the employer makes for the employee.

Years ago, as the insurance broker for a school district in southern Utah, I recommended that the school district provide annual benefit statements to its employees. The district was very generous with its benefits package, and the employer wanted to remind the teachers and other staff members of that fact. Besides paying all of the cost of the health insurance for the employees and their dependents, the district offered many additional employer-paid insurance benefits and a generous retirement plan.

The teacher's union, however, objected to the annual statements. The union leaders worried that if the employees saw the comprehensive list of benefits, they would think that all of those district-provided perks or allowances were part of their total compensation. The union's position was that employees were not being compensated fairly and that listing all the benefits the employees received was counterproductive to the union's cause. The school district and the teacher's union finally agreed to compromise: the district was allowed to show the employees the value of the private benefits, but none of the federal- or state-mandated programs could be included in their presentation.

Our insurance agency provides these benefit statements to our clients at no cost. It is just one way an employer can communicate the economic value of working for the company.

Chapter 12

Executive Planning

Failing to plan is planning to fail.

—*Alan Lakein*

Closely related to employee benefits is the special need for executive planning. This planning takes into consideration the possibility of losing officers and key employees, people who are vital to a company's success and upon whom the rest of the employees rely.

Companies can protect themselves against catastrophic events such as the death, disability, divorce or retirement of key persons (such as partners or stockholders). These protection plans even support the company's goals to attract and retain talented leadership.

Carefully executed legal documents, properly funded with insurance, will assure a bright future regardless of what lies ahead. This is basic risk management and a wise business practice.

When I was a boy, my parents owned a couple of Arctic Circle drive-in restaurants. They worked hard together and were able to provide themselves with a good living. Unfortunately, my father died prematurely when he was only 47. Although experienced in operating the company, my mother didn't have the expertise that my dad did. Unfortunately, there wasn't enough money available to hire an experienced manager. She closed one of the restaurants soon after he died, and she struggled to keep the other one open. Just a few years later, she closed it as well. All of their dreams for the future were gone.

Through proper executive planning, things might have been different.

A Perpetuation Plan

One way to protect the future of a company is through a *buy-sell agreement*. As the name implies, a buy-sell agreement is an agreement between the owners, partners, or shareholders of a closely held business about *buying and selling their interest in the business*. Specifically, each party pledges to offer his interest in the business to the others at a predetermined value if certain events occur (such as death, disability, divorce, retirement, resignation, or termination of employment).

The primary advantage of a buy-sell agreement is that the important decisions are made *before* there is a need to transfer one owner's business interests. This way, when a significant event occurs, the remaining owners can carry on the business without interruption. Typically, each party's spouse must sign off on the agreement in order to eliminate future disputes. In the absence of such an agreement, conflict will almost always arise—simply because there are competing interests and limited financial resources. Unfortunately, when money is involved, everyone tends to look out for himself.

As part of the pre-agreement process, many companies determine the value of their business. This can be done through an appraisal, or by using a formula commonly employed within their industry.

Personally, I have a buy-sell agreement in place for our insurance agency. It's important to me that not only will our clients be taken care of in my absence, but also that our employees will be too.

When presenting the need for a buy-sell agreement I often use the example of two partners, each of which owns half the business and both are married. If one of the partners dies, his or her spouse inherits their share of the business and then asks the remaining partner to buy out their interests.

But perhaps the surviving wife and the remaining partner can't agree on a price—or more likely, no money is available. The wife of the deceased partner is left owning half of a business. Is this a good scenario for either party?

Here is a twist on this fictional story. What if the wife of the deceased partner gets upset and decides to sell her interest in the company to a competitor? What is to stop her from doing so?

Or what if she decides to remarry, and her new husband wants to be involved in the business? Of course, the new spouse is prepared: he is in a business class in community college and knows all about running a company.

Certainly, some of these outcomes seem exaggerated, but there is always a risk.

Proper planning with the right insurance products reduces the financial risk of many unforeseen events. The owners of a business can create legal documents, and then purchase life and disability insurance to provide the money necessary to fulfill the terms of the agreement. The company can pay for the policies and have the other owner (or the business itself) be named as the policy owner and beneficiary. Additionally, permanent life insurance is a common financial vehicle that can also be used to accumulate equity or cash value for an eventual buy-out for needs other than death or disability.

A couple of years ago, I met with two sisters who owned a company they had acquired from their father. Although we gathered in order to discuss their commercial insurance needs, we also talked about their executive planning. I explained how a buy-sell agreement works and the advantages of having one.

After a long silence, they said that they wished they had known about a buy-sell agreement previously. One of the sisters was now divorced, and in the divorce decree, her ex-spouse was awarded half of her shares of the business. Now they had three owners of the business. One sister owns 50 percent, and the other sister and her ex-husband each own 25 percent of the company. Of course, the ex-spouse wants his share of the profits. Would a buy-sell agreement have helped this company?

The sisters recognized the value of executive planning for their business and scheduled an appointment to meet with their attorney to create a buy-sell agreement. They also purchased life insurance policies to provide the funding necessary to fulfill the buy-out obligations at death.

People Make All the Difference

Our agency recently obtained a Small Business Administration loan for expansion. In order to receive this loan, the bank required me to purchase a life insurance policy on my life with the lender named as the beneficiary. Apparently, the government assumes there is less likelihood it will be repaid if the principal of a business dies.

Key-person insurance, sometimes called "key man" insurance, protects a business in the event of the premature death or disability of an important asset—namely an individual necessary to the company's success. Companies routinely insure their buildings along with other real and personal property, so it makes sense to insure their most valuable assets: their key employees.

Every business has certain individuals who are essential to its success. Many times it is the president of the company, or an engineer, or a designer. For a construction firm a key person might be the company's estimator, because without a good estimator there are no jobs.

In almost every business, when certain people are necessary for the company to run profitably, the company may be at risk if they go out of the picture. A life and disability insurance policy can be purchased on those individuals, naming the business as the owner and beneficiary of the policy. Should something happen to these key persons, the business has the money to find replacements.

Investors, lenders, and clients are often put at ease when they know that protection is in place for the continuation of the business in the event that the firm loses a key employee.

I've had law firms purchase key-person policies on their partners, and businesses purchase life insurance policies on their top salespeople. Even if the business could survive the loss of a key employee, it may lose a substantial amount of income.

Besides the financial benefits of a key-person insurance policy, there are the psychological benefits for the team member. Everyone wants to be needed and feel valuable to others, and the business decision to purchase a life insurance policy on a key employee validates his self-worth and engenders his loyalty to the company.

In conversations with these key persons when they are applying for insurance, it is interesting to hear how they perceive their employer's efforts to insure their lives. Comments such as, "I guess they need me," and "Apparently the company thinks I'm important," are not unusual.

Other companies have found that permanent life insurance can be used to cover the calculated death benefit and provide a valuable non-qualified retirement program for their key person. Employers can give specific employees a reason to stay with the company for the long term. This concept has been referred to as "golden handcuffs," as a positive incentive for loyalty of service.

Conclusion

Thank you for taking the time to read this book. I hope that you, like many of the clients I have worked with, have found new ideas that will help you improve your overall employee benefits program. Perhaps you can think of others who can benefit from these concepts.

I realize that not all of these approaches will be new. Human resources professionals and others responsible for their company's employee benefits program will be familiar with some of the concepts discussed in this book. Some of these strategies have been in use by larger companies for some years now, and others are just becoming more popular as the provisions of the Affordable Care Act continue to affect employers. Nevertheless, I hope that you have been challenged and enlightened by the content herein.

I am grateful for the clients who have chosen to work with us to help them proactively manage their benefits programs. The majority of the companies we work with genuinely care about their employees and want to provide them the best benefits possible within the availability of their budget. Similarly, many clients have expressed their appreciation to me regarding the work our team does to assist them in meeting their human resource and financial goals. Together we form a partnership that enhances the lives of everyone involved.

Of course, every licensed insurance broker is entitled to the same premium rates from an insurance carrier. As I mentioned at the beginning of this book, while our agency can often save money for a company, sometimes it is more about having a *strategic partner* who is concerned about your company's success and can help you proactively manage your company's benefits program.

It has been my experience that many new clients have as much difficulty in changing insurance brokers as they do in changing their insurance policies and strategies. Following one of my seminars a while back, the controller of a large construction company approached me. She explained her company's problem: the company's long-time insurance broker was a friend of the owner's and old-fashioned in his approach. The controller explained that in all the years the business had purchased insurance through this agent, he had never suggested new ideas or strategies. At most, this agent simply shopped their policies once a year and tried to save a little money on renewal.

The company's controller particularly liked my suggestion of a health reimbursement arrangement, which she figured would save their company an estimated $23,000 a year and allow them to keep the same insurance carrier. The owner's biggest dilemma would be how to change brokers without offending her friend. I suggested a compromise: Make me their new insurance broker, implement the strategies had I presented, and send the other insurance agent a check for half of the savings. That way everybody would be happy!

The company agreed to work with me, and we implemented the plans I recommended, which saved the employer more than they had originally projected. I never did find out whether the owner sent the former insurance broker a check.

My team and I can produce similar strategies and results for your company. Please contact our office for a complimentary appointment. Elevate Insurance has the knowledge and resources to help you and your company move forward and meet the challenges of the future. I promise we will do our best to assist you in reaching your goals.

About the Author

Porter T. Talbot is the President and CEO of Elevate Insurance, an independent insurance agency in Las Vegas, Nevada, and executive director of The National Registry of Workers' Compensation Specialists. He is past president of the Boise, Idaho, and Central Utah Association of Insurance and Financial Advisors.

Porter graduated with a Master of Science in Financial Services degree from the American College in Bryn Mar, Pennsylvania, and a Bachelor of Science from the University of the State of New York. He holds several professional certifications including Chartered Life Underwriter (CLU), Chartered Financial Consultant (ChFC), Health Insurance Associate (HIA), and Registered Workers' Compensation Specialist (RWCS). He specializes in employee benefits, commercial insurance, and executive planning.

Porter shows his clients how to use creative strategies to enhance their employee benefits programs, save money, and improve morale. A gifted writer and speaker, Porter has shared his expertise through written material and speaking engagements.

Porter and his wife, Debbie, have been married for more than 30 years and have five children and ten grandchildren.